SEVEN YEARS
—— OF ——
TRIBULATION

SEVEN YEARS
—— OF ——
TRIBULATION

THE RESULT OF FALSE ALLEGATIONS

John D. Cadore

Seven Years of Tribulation

Copyright © 2020 by John D. Cadore. All rights reserved.

No part of this publication may be reproduced, stored in a retrieval system or transmitted in any way by any means, electronic, mechanical, photocopy, recording or otherwise without the prior permission of the author except as provided by USA copyright law.

The opinions expressed by the author are not necessarily those of URLink Print and Media.

1603 Capitol Ave., Suite 310 Cheyenne, Wyoming USA 82001
1-888-980-6523 | admin@urlinkpublishing.com

URLink Print and Media is committed to excellence in the publishing industry.

Book design copyright © 2020 by URLink Print and Media. All rights reserved.

Published in the United States of America

Library of Congress Control Number: 2021923601
ISBN 978-1-68486-036-4 (Paperback)
ISBN 978-1-68486-037-1 (Digital)

18.08.21

CONTENTS

DEDICATION 7
PREFACE 9
INTRODUCTION 11
1. WHY WAS I SINGLED OUT? 13
2. SEVEN YEARS OF TRIBULATION: THE STRUGGLES 15
3. THE IMPACT OF WRONGFUL PROSECUTION 17
4. THE ACTIONS OF THE STATE'S FIRST LEAD PROSECUTOR 21
5. THE IMPORTANCE OF HONESTY AND DOING WHAT IS RIGHT 23
6. DUTY TO MAKE WHOLE 25
7. THE EFFECTS OF THE LAST SEVEN YEARS UPON MY IMMEDIATE AND EXTENDED FAMILY 29
8. WHAT ROLES DO THOSE IN CIVIC DUTY AND CHURCH CONGREGATIONS HAVE TO EACH OTHER? 33
9. FAILURE OF DUTY TO MAKE WHOLE 35
10. JUDICIAL RETALIATION, REPRISAL, AND ABUSE OF POWER 37
11. IS JUSTICE COLOR-BLIND, OR IS JUSTICE DEFENDANT BLIND? 39
12. DUTY TO MAKE WHOLE: FACT OR FICTION 43
13. THE COVERUP CONTINUES: COMPLAINTS TO THE STATE COMMISSION ON JUDICIAL CONDUCT 45
14. LESSONS LEARNED 47

DEDICATION

The book is dedicated to my father, the late Fabian Patrick Cadore who passed away on Easter Sunday (Resurrection Sunday) on the 1st of April, 2018, at the tender age of one hundred (100). He was a very wise man, which led me to believe that wisdom and long life/longevity are very complementary.

PREFACE

It has been approximately seven years, since October 11, 2012, that the incident occurred which led me to write this book. This book entitled *Seven Years of Tribulation* is my seventh book written, but it will be the first published. The backdrop for all these seven books is the incident referred to above that occurred on October 11, 2012. To that date I had been a practicing attorney for several years as a solo practitioner in Binghamton, New York. My diligence and commitment to the highest levels of service to the Courts who gave me the work and the clients that I represented led me to receiving more work than any other Attorney in the assigned counsel system in Broome County, New York. As the person who received the most assignments in the County, it would be a mathematical certainty that my billing for doing the work for the most assignments in the County, and quite probably the State of New York, would most likely be the highest for attorneys participating in the program. Logic and mathematical certainty mean nothing or very little when political ends are being pursued instead of justice. It is somewhat amazing how certain incidents can and do arouse different senses, thoughts, and reflections of the human being.

It is with great relief that this book is being published today and not one or two years earlier. Today I can honestly say that I am no longer angry about what had occurred, and I am able to write this book with certain amount of peace and calm. It has taken me many years to really eliminate most or all my anger, which allowed me to write a somewhat impartial and objective book. Although this book may never obtain total impartiality, it has come a long way. This book is about the wrongful conduct of State and local government officials and employees, but after all, they are only humans.

It was not my intent to publish any book unless and until all litigation with the State of New York had concluded. However, litigation against the State of New York is lengthier and is more time consuming than was initially anticipated. Waiting until litigation is completed is no longer plausible. For instance, the mere length of time can have the effect of rendering the story cold and, by its very definition, less appealing to the public at large.

An additional reason for publishing this book, my seventh, before all others is because I am somewhat in love with the number seven. Biblically, seven is the number of completion. I am the seventh child in the family, and I was born in the seventh month. There is something about the number seven that is very appealing and attractive to me. It is my intent to publish a finished product that would hold and capture the reader's quest and imagination, and I am hoping that my goals have been achieved.

INTRODUCTION

There is an old saying, "Power corrupts, Absolute power corrupts absolutely". This expression, because of my recent experiences, has led me to believe it is absolutely true. It takes a special individual not to abuse his or her power when there is an abundance of power vested in him or her. But of course, Jesus was the only perfect individual to walk on the face of this earth.

What was the fate of Jesus? Foolish men that had a craving for power betrayed and crucified him. The maker of this world was crucified by men that were unable to save themselves. They were religious men with a craving for power. If such a thing was done to Jesus, what man is immune from foolish men seeking to display what little power they perceive themselves to have? The foolishness of man! However, in the case of Jesus, it was predestined to occur as the ransom or price for the sins of man. The real-life characters in the pages to follow can lay no claim to divinity or higher moral purposes for the actions that they took.

This book is intended to convey to the reader that public officials and government employees, unless checked and/or scrutinized, may and many times do take certain actions to benefit themselves and their individual self-interests in direct conflict with the laws that they have sworn to uphold. To that end, the Founding Fathers displayed great vision when they designed a governmental system with checks and balances. Without checks and balances, there may be the tendency to usurp each other's power, governmental function, and authorities. The need for man to stroke his ego is great, therefore in the absence of proper checks and balances, we may, or could, in the end have an ineffective system of government.

No one is above the law, and everyone should be held responsible for their action. The county executive or the attorney general that is willing to do almost anything to boost their political standing is not above the law and should be held accountable for their actions.

CHAPTER ONE

WHY WAS I SINGLED OUT?

Of all the attorneys that worked for the State of New York Attorneys for Children Program assigned counsel panel and the County of Broome assigned counsel program, why was I singled out?

As a black Naturalized American Citizen, the cloud of prejudice apparent from this political prosecution is unmistakable.

The reason is solely because I worked longer hours, had more cases, and I believe I had more difficult cases than most of the other attorneys in those programs. Having the largest caseload and working the most hours would more than likely also translate into the highest paid attorney in the program. If you work more hours than anyone else in a program, you are paid more than anyone else in the program who has not worked as much as you have. During the pretrial period, before my case was heard by the jury and I was acquitted, I asked the attorney for the state attorney general's office prosecuting the criminal case how many cases had been handled during the time period in question, from 2009 to 2012. To this she answered, "I do not know." To this day, the office prosecuting the criminal charge has not been able to give me an answer. To bring a criminal case for fraud when you do not know what is the numerical basis for the charge is the clearest indication of a political prosecution that there can be.

That answer was a total shock to me because how could anyone be charged with overbilling for legal work performed if the accusers were unaware of the number of cases involved?

This was a political witch hunt spearheaded by an Attorney General who left office amid a scandal of sexual misconduct and alleged drug usage. If the State were to be given the benefit of the doubt that they were telling the truth and they did not know how many cases were being handled by me in the time period covered in their investigative accounting, they clearly had not done an accurate review of the facts. Accounting is not a social science. It is hard numbers. To base a criminal prosecution on not knowing hard numbers is exactly what a political witch hunt looks like. After the close of the criminal trial, it was clear that the jury agreed that without real numbers, this was simply a political witch hunt. One member of the jury expressed to me, after the reading of the verdict, that another jury member had said, "He is not owing the State of New York any money, instead the State of New York owes him."

My case was heard by an all-white jury. To this fact, I was very uneasy about the racial overtones, knowing the extent of racism within this country. My takeaway from this ordeal is that there are many people in New York State and in the United States of America, that should a black and foreign-born attorney earn more than his white natural-born counterparts, then the black attorney is doing something illegal or has done something wrong.

It is my belief that State of New York knew that their conduct was wrongful and were trying to cover up their wrongful actions by desperately seeking to take a settlement of this case. A settlement of this case? Absolutely not. That I wanted no part of. I knew I was innocent and wanted to prove it. I do not believe the State of New York envisioned a trial. It is my belief that they were doing whatever they could to have me plead guilty to some crime so that they would not have to go through a show trial.

It is my belief that some State officials and high-ranking State employees were envisioning rising up the political ladder with a victory of any kind in my case. The attorney general of New York State made a personal appearance to Broome County on the day of the jury verdict. It is my belief that he was attempting to raise his political stock. He was silent about the jury's verdict.

During the course of the political prosecution, the State removed me from panels upon which I had previously served. Then they refused to pay vouchers for time already spent. It is my belief that these steps were taken so that I would not be able to afford to go to trial in the matter. My innocence and reliance on the inherent justice of our criminal system of law refused me the conscience to plead guilty to anything which I had not done.

The weakness of the case had been disclosed by the first prosecutor in the case, who applied for a position in a different section of the attorney general's office prior to the trial. The first prosecutor indicated that she was unsure whether charges would or should be brought but indicated that she was being pressured to file charges by certain individuals from Broome County.

Earlier, I mentioned that as a result of the charges, I was removed from all panels giving assigned counsel work. The State was seeking to ensure that my stream of income was stopped, rendering my ability to effectively defend myself eviscerated. These steps left me without income for the work that had been duly performed and authorized.

Lack of income is probably the most significant tribulation most people probably suffer in their lifetimes. Lack of income coupled with wrongful impugning of professional reputation is insult to injury— injury inflicted wrongly by those who had sworn an oath to know and to do differently but chose to willingly throw their moral standards to the wind for possible political gain.

Through all of this, I persevered.

CHAPTER TWO

SEVEN YEARS OF TRIBULATION: THE STRUGGLES

It was on the tenth of October 2012 that a City of Binghamton City court judge signed a search warrant authorizing the search of my law office and confiscation of 344 of my client files, On or about October 11, 2012, marked the beginning of my and my family's seven years of tribulation. Today on July 22, 2019, I have a civil suit pending against the State of New York. Among other things, this action is seeking damages for slander, libel, defamation of character, destruction of my business's good name, and destruction of my law practice.

In October 2012, at the beginning of my seven years of tribulation, I never foresaw or envisioned myself suing the State of New York and having my case heard in the highest court in the State. No one could have predicted the lengths that the court system has gone to try to overturn a jury verdict of not guilty in a matter that should have never been brought in the first place.

My story has a somewhat Shakespearian feel to it. The New York Court of Appeals is the very same court that recently rendered a groundbreaking decision that President Donald J. Trump can be personally sued by individuals or entities during his tenure as president of the United States. It is my opinion that this is a political decision. President Donald J. Trump's former Democratic buddies have now decided, after losing their effort to elect Hilary Clinton at the voting booths of the country, to seek political justice not with the voters but within the smoky backrooms of courthouses outside the watch of public pressure.

Please note that I am not a Republican or a Democrat. I am the longest tenured independent voter that I know. I have been an independent voter long before H. Ross Perot made his bid for the presidency of the United States as independent.

The reason for saying that President Donald J. Trump's buddies have now decided to turn on him is because in his former younger years, President Donald J. Trump was a card-carrying registered Democrat.

My case, which was before the New York State Court of Appeals, is seeking monetary damages for the wrongful criminal prosecution commenced in 2012 by the New York State attorney general's office. The basis for my lawsuit seeking a default judgment against the State of New York is based upon the State's failure to answer my duly filed and duly served claim that was legally served upon the New York State Office of the Attorney General on May 30, 2017. New York State failed to answer the duly filed and duly served complaint/claim.

This book, *Seven Years of Tribulation*, is actually my seventh book written since the beginning of my ordeal that began back on October 11, 2012. This is my first book to be published. This book has allowed me to give my readers an overview of the ordeals of deliberate wrongful acts by government officials and the effect that dedicated wrongful persecution can have on a person's quality of life and standard of living, together with the effect it has on one's family and others who have tried to help right the wrongs of seven years of knowingly made criminal acts by state officials of the court system.

Most significantly, when one is wrongfully accused, the end result is a political prosecution with individuals whose goals are to cover up the facts in order to protect themselves, their reputations, and their careers. Any type of legal proceeding can be very costly; however when legal proceedings are based upon knowingly false information and prosecuted by persons lacking the moral fortitude to stand up for the truth in the process of the administration of justice, the damages are simply greater and more morally heinous.

Earlier, I mentioned that this is my seventh book of pen to paper but the first of word to the printer's press. This book attempts to show from the perspective of seven years' reflection, an overview of a system sworn to truth and justice which has gone knowingly and horribly damagingly wrong.

The Court of Appeals, in their decision, held that the "motion is dismissed upon the ground that the order sought to be appealed from does not finally determine the action within the meaning of the Constitution." A ruling of default is dispositive of an action. Therefore, by failing to make a ruling, the Court of Appeals has undermined the principle of judicial economy, which in layman's language, is "justice delayed is justice denied."

The goal of this book is to provide readers with a brief overview of what the personal and professional damages of knowingly improper state action can be. It is also intended to inform readers that public employees and civil servants are no different from members of the society at large, even if they have sworn an oath to uphold the very law that they break. The state officials in this story are imperfect individuals that make mistakes and bad decisions, just like everyone else in society.

CHAPTER THREE

THE IMPACT OF WRONGFUL PROSECUTION

Criminal prosecution, whether wrongfully or rightfully prosecuted, has numerous side effects. One of the most significant impacts of any prosecution is employment implications. Even though I remain self-employed, the effects of criminal prosecution for political purposes still has a significant and, in most instances, negative effect of one's business, employment, and eventual job searches.

Being a private practitioner, the most significant impact I have observed thus far is a tremendous reduction of the amount of new and former clients contacting my office for legal services. It constitutes the most severe form of slander, libel, and defamation of character, destruction of business reputation, and the loss of good name earned over the professional lifetime of decades of private practice law business. This is more so when libel, slander, and defamation of character are committed by unethical public servants seeking to make a name for themselves at any cost.

In my case, the dramatic irony is that both of the key political players primarily responsible for my wrongful prosecution tragedy were forced out of public office in criminal disgrace. Attorney General Eric Schneiderman left his gleaming offices overlooking the lowly citizens, whom he lorded over from the top floor of every state office building, in shame over immoral sex acts with willing partners eager to climb the ladder of governmental success through whatever means they could use—their bodies, not their brains, being the most frequently used, and sexual abuse. The other politician instrumental in the criminal prosecution was the Broome County executive Debbie Preston. Ms. Preston was arrested as she left office after an election loss and later plead guilty to unlawful use of municipal Credit Cards. Ms. Preston misused or embezzled public funds entrusted to her.

What a Dramatic Irony in the Allegations Made against Me

On August 14, 2014, the New York State attorney general Eric Schneiderman held a press conference on the doorsteps of the attorney general's office in Albany to announce to the world that I had overbilled the State of New York and the County of Broome for legal services provided to individuals in an amount of about ($10,000) ten thousand. The question any reasonable person should have asked themselves is, Why would a lawyer with over twenty years of legal practice defraud the State of New York and the County of Broome ten thousand dollars? Such allegation should be considered laughable by any individual of average intelligence.

Shortly after the Binghamton City court judge signed the court warrant for the seizure of client files from my office, it became a topic of discussion between myself and certain members of the local bar association. I can recall saying to all who would listen that I had no cause for concern about the State being in possession of 344 of my client files because I knew that they would find there was no wrong doing on my behalf and they would eventually have to return all of my files. One local attorney's response to me was "John, you are mistaking things. They will find something. They have to find somethings wrong. Otherwise they will be faced with a major lawsuit." That local attorney was correct.

According to other local attorneys, the New York State attorney general's office is aware of that, so they must find a wrongful act was committed.

Amid all the State's false and scandalous allegations made against me, on at least one occasion, I can recall asking the assistant attorney general prosecuting the matter, "Within the period that I was accused of committing wrongful acts, what was the total number of cases that had been handled by me for the various courts and judges served by me on the assignment panels?" The prosecuting assistant attorney general answered me that she did not know how many cases had been handled by me. How can a prosecution based on overbilling not be based upon a very specific knowledge of the number of cases that are within the window of the conduct charged? It is my belief that the reason the lead prosecutor for the State had to lie and say that she did not know how many cases I handled during the period from January 2009 to September 2011 period was because I handled at least twice as many cases as most of the other attorneys for the State of New York and County of Broome during the time period in question. It is only logical that with today's high technology data collection and retrieval that the State of New York knew exactly the number of cases that had been handled by me. The State was embarrassed to tell the truth and instead said that they did not know the amount of cases I handled during the period from January 2009 to September 2011. Hence, in order to cover up their dishonesty and lies, the State could only tell yet another lie.

It is also my belief that the State never intended this case to go to trial, or in short, be tried in front of a jury in a court of law. The tactics of the State were to intimidate and threaten the single defendant against the power of the State to capitulate to something he did not do. A guilty plea would have allowed them the political capital they were seeking in this witch hunt.

Upon Execution of the Search Warrant on or about October 11, 2012

Immediately upon the execution of the search warrant on my law office, the very first action taken by both the State of New York and County of Broome was to stop assigning me new cases and to reassign all my existing clients and open files to other attorneys participating in the attorney assignment programs involved.

It is also my belief that the primary reason for such actions was to limit my ability to earn an income, thus rendering it virtually impossible for me to adequately defend myself against the power of the State in a court of law. At the very same time, as they cut off my source of income, they were telling lies to every press outlet locally and throughout the State, knowing slander, libel, and defamation of character. There are few things that can tarnish a reputation more than a headline of indictment for lying, cheating, and stealing. All these acts were intentional and done with motive to financially destroy me before the trial. Innocent until proven guilty is not a legal construct that was being adhered to by the attorney general's office in this case.

The truth does not yield to lies. The State's belief that their presentation of knowing lies to the jury would carry the day was not very wise. The jury was able to recognize their falsehood.

CHAPTER FOUR

THE ACTIONS OF THE STATE'S FIRST LEAD PROSECUTOR

Approximately one and a half years after the State of New York and law enforcement individuals seized 344 of my clients' files and about one and a half years into the investigation, the then lead prosecuting attorney revealed to my initial attorney, an attorney that I replaced because I was displeased with the Service provided that "she was unsure if any charges would be brought against me, but she is being forced to bring charges by two individuals from Broome County".

According to my first attorney, he was informed by the State lead prosecutor that she was unsure if any charges should even be pursued or that she would bring forth any charges, but she was being forced to bring charges against me by certain individuals in Broome County.

About six months after this revelation to my first criminal attorney, I learned that she was no longer the lead prosecutor in my case and that a different attorney would be assigned to prosecute or handle the case. It was my understanding that she moved from the criminal prosecution branch of the attorney general's office to the civil prosecution branch of the office. In the vast majority of instances, the only reason for criminal prosecutors to leave a prosecution is that there is no legitimate case to be made against the defendant. That was the case here.

It is also worth mentioning that both of the political kingpins in the prosecution, New York State Attorney Eric Schneiderman and County Executive Debbie Preston, were up for reelection. As noted earlier, this case was a political prosecution aimed at bolstering political careers, not in any way furthering the public good. Prosecutions based upon feeding the ambition of elected officials and prosecutions not based upon the accurate facts against citizens being charged will always fail.

Attorney General Schneiderman's misdeeds are now public record, as he lounges in retirement after slithering from his office in disgrace and scandal. He was forced out of office in the middle of a scandal involving sexual misconduct and drug allegations.

County Executive Preston plead guilty to One Count of OFFICIAL MISCONDUCT for stealing public property as she left her elected office after losing her election. Precisely what she wrongfully accused me of doing, the passage of time exposed the true nature of the person intricately involved in my prosecution.

CHAPTER FIVE

THE IMPORTANCE OF HONESTY AND DOING WHAT IS RIGHT

My deceased father, before passing at the age of one hundred, once told me "that it is much better when people do wrong to you than when you do wrong to others." He emphasized that very much and told me that I should never forget that. He also told me that "wrongful deeds committed would always bring or cause regrets." Although we are nothing but mere mortal men, we should make every attempt to do what is right or correct.

My recent and ongoing experience is that we should always at least try our best to do what is right because by so doing we are able to defend ourselves to the end. The only reason I am able to boldly and proudly sue the State of New York and stand ready to take whatever steps are necessary to ensure that justice is done and that justice will prevail is because there exists no doubt or questions in my mind that I committed any wrongful acts.

In my recent Motion to the Court of Appeals, I pointed out the facts and law to The Court. The brief was very pleasing to me and upon completion of that short brief to the Court of Appeals, it dawned on me that it is one of the best briefs I had written throughout my entire legal career.

The attorney general's response to my brief to the New York State Court of Appeals, although not shocking, was somewhat surprising. The State of New York never responded or attacked the merits of the brief but instead asked the Court of Appeals not to hear the matter because it was not final. Hence, this matter is still pending and active in a lower court.

After all, the attorney general's office was charged with the pursuit of justice for all its citizens. This is also the New York State Court of Appeals, the highest court in the state of New York. The matter before the court was a motion for default judgment that the court refused to rule on, passing the decision back to a lower court. That action by the Court of Appeals simply flies in the face of the principles of stare decisis and the law as enacted by the assembly and senate of the State of New York and signed into law by the governor. The court cannot ignore the law that it does not want to enforce.

The actions of the attorney general's office by asking the Court of Appeals to not decide the matter is contrary to the interests of justice and the law as embodied in the acts of the legislature signed into law by the governor. Following the law should be the first and only priority of the court. The attorney general's position of justice delayed is only justice denied. The attorney general's actions and arguments reveal that their primary concern was not the administration of justice for all but rather to protect the reputation and face of the other elected and appointed officials in the public domain. The court has taken a knowing step from its sworn duty to uphold the law and deliver justice for the citizens and litigants in the court system of the State of New York.

The notion of judicial economy is likewise not applicable here. By erasing the concept of default from the administration of civil justice, the court has only swung open the doors for thousands of new judges to make rulings in matters upon which no controversy exists. The attorney general's asking the court to erase default from civil pleadings is the greatest waste of public resources for precious and expensive time of judicial officials that can be imagined. The attorney general's office, by asking the court to not hear or decide on the default motion, is saying to the court, "We do not care how much of our time, or any other Court's time, is taken by this matter. All we desire is to have things the way we think they should be." A default from May of 2017 still hanging around twenty-six months later is not the swift and efficient administration of justice.

Could the actions of the attorney general's office in this matter signal their mistrust or lack of confidence in the Court of Appeals? Advocating for the highest court to make rules that create thousands of new jobs for literally cases that are in civil default does a disservice to the citizens and taxpayers of the State of New York.

CHAPTER SIX

DUTY TO MAKE WHOLE

The duty to make whole is a concept or notion derived from the common law whereby after any prosecution or court action in a criminal case, the party doing the wrong act is to restore the injured party to wholeness, as if the act had not been committed. The defendant was acquitted in a criminal trial; his restoration to the position enjoyed by him prior to the filing of the charges is the very basic measure of fairness afforded to him. This is an equitable concept wholly adopted in all other areas of the law, from contract to domestic relations. The concept to return or restore the lesser economically advantaged spouse to the same living conditions or similar living conditions that were enjoyed during the marriage is a bedrock principal of fairness and equity. This is accomplished by court awards of alimony or child support each and every day that the courts are open for business in the State of New York and throughout the country.

After my acquittal in October of 2015, both the State of New York and the County of Broome had the legal duty to make reasonable efforts to restore me to the same or similar economic position enjoyed by me prior to the commencement of the political prosecution. Fairness would dictate payment for past services rendered and not paid, as well as restoration to the panels of attorneys doing the work for the court system.

Neither the State of New York nor the County of Broome ever took one step to right the wrongs done. My suspicion is that both entities were and still are trying their utmost best to cover up and ignore the knowing wrong committed by them in the name of the people of the State of New York. They are trying to sweep everything under the rug and hope that the public would believe them and that I would simply vanish.

Not only did they fail to do what was the right and legally correct thing to do, but in order to protect their public jobs, their professional careers, and their publicly funded retirements, they went one step further. This time they made a complaint against me to an administrative body, the attorney grievance committee, appointed by the people who committed the wrong, who are only answerable to the people that committed the wrong and have no accountability to the public for their actions. As stated earlier, the complaint to the ethics committee was their final step to cover up themselves now faced with a substantial lawsuit. Like the first action that resulted in a failed political prosecution, the second attempt to cover also failed, and they are now faced with a lawsuit showing the terrible misdeeds of unelected officials against innocent, by criminal jury verdict, citizens.

The lawsuit against the State and the County was originally filed and served in 2017. The County was released from the Court of Claims action, citing the principle that the Court of Claims' sole jurisdiction is for claims against the State. Interestingly, instead of transferring the claim to the proper forum, which is what the Court procedurally was supposed to have done, they simply dismissed the County as a party to the lawsuit.

The notion of substantial participation is derived from the legal principle of pendent jurisdiction. Pursuant to the principle of pendent jurisdiction, whenever the underlying facts and transactions occurred together or are significantly linked, then it is proper for the same court, or a single court, to decide the matter.

A good explanation of this principle can be found in the US Supreme Court. The US Supreme Court does not express jurisdiction over family court matters or family law, but some of the most farreaching and substantial decisions in family law came from the US Supreme Court. That is because whenever a case is before the US Supreme Court, the entire case is usually decided. This, in my opinion, is a very good thing.

One good reason for pendent jurisdiction is the notion of judicial economy. The principles of judicial economy and interests of justice to me are very much interrelated. The principle of judicial economy is why within the criminal legal system we have the plea bargain. One of the main reasons for offering a plea bargain is to reduce the amount of cases that have to be tried, thereby freeing the court's time to deal with the more serious or controversial cases.

The concept of interests of justice can be best described as justice delayed is justice denied. Back to the case at bar, this was my argument to the court why the trial court should not have released the County of Broome as a defendant in the matter. Of course, I am talking about principles of law, but this case constitutes the application of the law as written to the facts as presented. The handling of this case should mirror the principles of law as carried forward from our Founding Fathers to this day of fairness, justice, and equity. This case shows the corruption of the lofty principles of the law for the vain and shallow promotion of individuals to the next rung up on the ladder and not the greater interests of justice for all in the society. The actions of the elected and appointed officials seeking to not have personal responsibility placed upon them for knowing wrongs that they have committed are wrong in every sense of the word. The officials are trying to protect themselves as not being the individual or person directly responsible for the bad acts of the state and the monetary damages it has caused. Of course, there is also one last piece to this puzzle—Broome County is not a large place, and the trial judge is a political appointee. We all know instances where politics has triumphed or overruled the higher ideals of justice.

The bottom line in this matter is that my argument to keep Broome County as a defendant in this batter failed because according to the trial judge, the Court of Claims was an improper forum to sue the County. Only New York State can be sued in the Court of Claims. I disagree because the incident or incidences that gave rise to this legal action occurred during the same transaction or transactions, and the County of Broome was a party to it. Therefore, using this notion of pendent jurisdiction, the County should also be a party to this action. However, I am not the judge, and the judge's decision must stand, unless or until it is appealed and the higher court rules otherwise or reverses the lower court's decision.

All the reasons mentioned within this chapter explained why this is my seventh book written concerning this matter but is the first to publication.

CHAPTER SEVEN

THE EFFECTS OF THE LAST SEVEN YEARSUPON MY IMMEDIATE AND EXTENDED FAMILY

Despite the severe financial hardship cast upon my family over the last seven years, my children have excelled in all their academic and extracurricular activities. Both of my children have graduated from college with honors in very marketable degrees. My youngest son graduated with a degree in finance, logistics, and transportation, and my oldest son graduated with two degrees and a minor. My oldest earned a degree in biomedical engineering, a degree in chemistry, and a minor in mathematics. He intends to pursue a PhD in biomedical engineering and to attend medical school. My youngest son is a Military Officer, as I was a Commissioned Officer both in the Texas Army National Guard and the New York Army National Guard before practicing law. I am trying my best to convince my youngest son to attend law school, but it's my belief that because of my experience in the legal system, he is having second thoughts about attending law school. It's my belief that my experience has left a nasty taste in his mouth, but I believe that it is up to me to convince him that within all professions, there are individuals that are willing to make a name for themselves by stepping on the backs of others and not by reaching down to give them a helping hand up the ladder. This, however, should not deter anyone from choosing any particular profession.

This is one reason why it is very important to me to be victorious in my lawsuits against the State of New York. To enable my son to see that, like the great Reggae singer Bob Marley once said, "it takes a small axe to cut down a big tree." Additionally, being versed in the law and the legal system is of great assistance when dealing with any type of injustice and overreaching by individuals in any profession or walk of life. Despite the adversity thrust upon me and my family over the past seven years, my children have excelled significantly. Maybe the adversity could be a blessing in disguise.

However, the flip side of that is due to the financial hardship heaped upon my family over the last seven years, I was unable to spend the time with my father as I really desired or wanted to. It was my intention to spend much more time with my father during his later years. Spending time with my father, in my case, always or usually results not only in more togetherness between us, but it usually yields lots of wisdom, information, and insights that I never knew or heard of before. This has been one of the main pitfalls or drawbacks of the last seven years.

My father resided on the island of Grenada, where he died on April 1, 2018. He died on Easter Sunday, Resurrection Day, at the age of one hundred. Although he was given the blessing of a very long life, people in his home community who knew him for many years and were familiar with his life and family history attested that my dad was actually between 105 and 110 years of age when he passed away. One of my father's friends, ninety-five himself, born and raised and still in our ancestral home village on Grenada, swears that he remembered my dad as a grown man in his life before this now ninety-five-year old man was the age of ten. My father's friend swore that my father had to have been at least 110 years of age at the time of his passing.

A stranger, or someone that is unfamiliar with the way people in developing countries once lived, may ask, "How is it possible for such a thing to occur?" Why are so many people saying that my father was so much older than one hundred years upon his passing? The answer to this question is not complicated. At the time of my father's birth, people were not preoccupied with the date of birth. Age was not that important to them. Most of the village men were either farmers or fishermen. Their primary concern was being able to provide for their families. The date of birth of a child during those years was not given as a top priority. Because of this reason, it was not uncommon to not register the birth of a child for a long time after the actual birth. Additionally, my father's family resided in a small village several miles from the capital of the island and a few miles from the capital of the parish the family resided. During those times, it was also not uncommon for a neighbor or family member to register the birth of the child whenever they went to the capital or were not too busy attending the immediate needs of the family. In lots of instances, the child was given the date of birth when the parents or family member or family friend actually registered the child into the government records, not at the actual date of birth of the child. This scenario was not uncommon throughout many developing countries of the world.

I can recall this scenario occurring in the World Little League competition approximately five years ago. My recollection is that it occurred with a boy that was born in the Dominican Republic and was playing baseball for a team in the Bronx in New York City. The player in question was accused of being much older than his certificate revealed. Some people referred to this scenario as cheating, but because of my knowledge of children's dates of birth registration in many developing countries, I immediately understood how such a scenario is highly probable and maybe possible in that incident referenced.

My Very First Immigration Case

During my tenure at law school, I was very interested in immigration law. Thus, every semester during my third year of law school, I enrolled either in an immigration law course or an immigration law clinic. While a third year law student enrolled in an immigration law clinic, I was tasked with obtaining a work permit for an immigrant from the island of Haiti. This was my first encounter with such a situation; the individual that I was representing or assisting did not have a birth certificate. He needed affidavits from friends, family members, and from people who knew him for several years to attest for him. This situation or problem is also not uncommon in many developing countries.

CHAPTER EIGHT

WHAT ROLES DO THOSE IN CIVIC DUTYAND CHURCH CONGREGATIONS HAVE TO EACH OTHER?

I was born and raised a Roman Catholic. Any and all significant spiritual and Christian activity in my life took place in the Roman Catholic Church. Until I immigrated to the US in 1979, I predominantly attended Catholic schools. At one point in my life, I seriously contemplated becoming a Roman Catholic priest. However, until my seven years of tribulation, there may have been some characteristics, traits, or behaviors within the Roman Catholic Church that perhaps I was blind to.

One of such characteristics, traits, or behaviors is the civil duty that each church member or congregation member has to each other. I would love to hear from maybe other denominations about the civic duty or ethical behavior that is biblically established by other faithful followers about their duty, responsibilities, or ethical behaviors to other members of their individual congregations to each other.

This topic is of great importance to me because a reasonable number of people that were and are significantly involved in my failed political prosecution not only were members of the Roman Catholic Church but are members or parishioners of the same churches that I attended.

It is written in the Bible that "many are called, but few are chosen." What are the characteristics of the chosen few?

CHAPTER NINE

FAILURE OF DUTY TO MAKE WHOLE

In October 2012, the State of New York wrongfully obtained a warrant signed by a Binghamton City court judge and seized 344 of my clients' files from my law office. I was wrongfully and maliciously accused of overbilling the State of New York and County of Broome for law guardian / attorney for the children's cases and assigned counsel cases for adult clients. These wrongful accusations resulted in a one-week trial in Broome County Court from October 19, 2015, to October 23, 2015. I was acquitted of all charges by jury verdict. Some members of the jury, after the conclusion of the case, expressed shock and disbelief of the actions taken by the State in the prosecution. It was a failed political prosecution, championed by the local county executive who was trying to boost her political currencies and rise up the political ladder.

As stated earlier in this book, many of the players in this failed political prosecution have lived to see their evil twist back and bite them. Former New York State Attorney General Eric Schneiderman, one of the key players, was forced to resign from his post as attorney general amid serious scandals of drug abuse and sexual misconduct. Broome County Executive Debbie Preston, perhaps the greatest advocate for the prosecution in the first place, was arrested during the later part of her term as Broome County Executive for embezzling and misappropriating public funds entrusted to her. There were other public employees involved in the criminal prosecution who retired or sought different employment since the conclusion of my case.

Why did all those public officials decide to pick me as their scapegoat? That answer is simple. At the time, I was the highest paid attorney in Broome County that served on the various state and county assigned counsel panels. The fact that I am a black man and an immigrant cannot be overlooked either. Combining all those factors, the politicians driving the prosecution clearly thought they had an easy mark, which would both in the long and the short term bolster their political standings.

After my acquittal, a few months later, I wrote and addressed an identical letter to three of the highest ranking judges in the State of New York that were either directly involved in my case or in the direct chain of command in the State Court system. I expressed to them how shocked and surprised I was by the actions undertaken by them against me. In that very letter, I respectfully asked for the following:

1. Recession of their letters/orders prohibiting me from being paid for work that been performed and was unbilled.

2. Reinstatement to all assigned counsel panels on which I had been a member.

3. Copy me in on the letters noted in numbers 1 and 2.

The silence from the failure of the duly elected and appointed judicial officers to do the right thing was and still is deafening. No attempt at restoration has ever been taken.

My same written requests for reinstatement were made to all appropriate agencies within the State from whom I had ever received work. No response from anyone.

The actions of the public officials of ignoring the requests are greater violations of our common moral and ethical code than the failed prosecution. By not complying with the law, they are directly saying that "they are above the law." They act as if the judgment of a jury of their peers has no binding effect on their actions. They will do as they see fit, not as is written in the law. It has been said that what you do speaks so loud that it drowns out what you say. The actions of the public officials herein are screaming corruption of the most basic and perverse level while lifting up the nonuniform enforcement of the law. These officials are above the law and immune to consequences for their knowing bad acts. The only message expressed here is that everyone else within the State of New York must comply with these laws, but not us. They are above the law and they are immune.

After my acquittal in my criminal case, the State had a legal duty to make me whole. Making someone whole means to restore the individual to the position or lifestyle that individual enjoyed prior to the legal action being taken against them. In my case, not only did the State of New York refuse to make me whole, but they instead utilized all sorts of vindictive measures against me with the direct intent of destroying my business and professional reputation.

CHAPTER TEN

JUDICIAL RETALIATION, REPRISAL, AND ABUSE OF POWER

This chapter might better be titled "Crooks in High Places." On October 11, 2012, the date my seven years of tribulation began, I had more than a hundred completed and unbilled cases for the various assigned counsel panels as well as more than a hundred incomplete and unbilled matters on which substantial legal work was performed. The open cases were taken away from me and assigned to other attorneys to complete.

After my acquittal, I was restored to the Tioga County assigned counsel panel and began receiving assignments from a few small town and village courts. This was brought to an abrupt end when the newly retired chief judge of the Appellate Division Third Department, Hon. Karen Peters, made a phone call to the chief administrative Broome County Supreme Court judge, telling her to call Tioga County and inform them that they should stop assigning any more cases to me. This action was clearly taken without giving it a second thought or even thinking of according me even the most elemental aspect of our system of due process in justice—notice. The effect of the person at the top of the ladder ordering something to be done cannot be understated. The failure of the presiding judge to respect the jury's verdict and the requirements of the law thereafter is symbolic of a greater disrespect for the sanctity of the rule of law than anything. The actions of the judge removing me, after acquittal, from panels which had been faithfully served by me for decades prior to the seven years of tribulation is wrong in every sense of the word.

As a former commissioned and non-commissioned military officer, one of the things that was frequently discussed among us was carrying out an illegal order and the consequences for partaking in such actions. The question that I have repeatedly asked myself is whether military officers adhere to a higher code of ethics than New York State judges. Actions speak louder than words. Even as an enlisted soldier, rank E-5 in the US Army, we were always very concerned with and were alert to not carry out illegal orders. Does an enlisted soldier in the US Army adhere to a higher standard than a New York State judge? Actions speak louder than words.

CHAPTER ELEVEN

IS JUSTICE COLOR-BLIND, OR IS JUSTICE DEFENDANT BLIND?

The standard of the law is to not let color affect the judgment of the decision maker but to only rely on the facts. The New York State Court system, sadly, has turned their back on this underlying principle of fairness. I appealed to the Third Department, Appellate Division of the Supreme Court of the State of New York, however my case was transferred to the Fourth Department, Appellate Division of the Supreme Court of the State of New York. Despite a ruling by the trial judge that the respondent failed to answer the petition/claim, the court ruled that there was no default in pleading. According to the court, the State of New York answered by claim/complaint on May 4, 2017. The court made this finding despite being presented with an affidavit of service that clearly showed that service upon the State was effected on May 30, 2017. An affidavit of service is a legal document that must be filed with the court whenever a party to a lawsuit is served with a summons and complaint or claim in matters involving the government. In my case, there was only one affidavit of service which accompanied the May 30, 2017, service upon the State of New York.

The CPLR, which is the Civil Practice Law and Rules, are the rules governing the civil practice of law in the state of New York.

The tale continues with the Appellate Division's sua sponte, on their own motion, with notice to the parties, transferring the case to the Appellate Division Fourth Department for a ruling. To the best of my knowledge, there is no procedure given in the CPLR or by the legislature in the law for the transfer of a matter from one Appellate Division to another. However, such action is proper to avoid the appearance of conflict of interest or the appearance of partiality.

Despite the court record showing only one affidavit of service stating clearly that service upon the State was effectuated on May 30, 2017, and that the legislature had spoken on the issue through CPLR 4516, the court chose to ignore the law and hold that the State had answered a summons and complaint served on the State on May 4, 2017. No system of justice can have public credibility when the facts and the law are ignored by the judges presiding over it.

The Fourth Department's February 2019 decision, which stated that the State of New York had timely answered the summons and complaint, was promptly appealed to the New York State Court of Appeals. The Court of Appeals is the highest state court.

A motion was made to the Court of Appeals seeking to reverse the Appellate Division's decision that the State had not defaulted in their reply to the summons and complaint that had been duly served upon them on May 30, 2017.

The May 13, 2019, decision of the Court of Appeals held:

> Appellant having moved for the Court of Appeals; upon the papers filed and due deliberation, it is ORDERED that the motion is dismissed upon the ground that the order sought to be appealed from does not finally determine the action within the meaning of the Constitution.

In everyday language, the highest court in the State refused to decide on whether the State had defaulted in pleading, after the trial-level judge had made a specific finding that the State had defaulted in pleading. To quote old literary references and authors, how Orwellian can this be? The year 1984 was more than thirty years ago, but the logic, or clear lack thereof, applied by the highest court in the State is befuddling.

One of the former foundations of New York law is that deference is to be given to the first decision rendered by the first judge that had the opportunity to rule on the matter. The Latin term *stare decisis* is what was taught in law school. To rule against well-established and settled law and legal principles creates laws that are never final and are always subject to whatever political wind is blowing when the sun comes up each morning.

In the rare or far-fetched chance that justice is indeed color-blind, one must then ask questions, "Is justice money blind?" Are individuals awarded the same or proportional or similar justice despite the deepness of their pocket or the standing or social position of the plaintiff or defendant? Would an individual receive equal justice against the State of New York as against Joe No Name Smith?

When the question is asked, "Is justice really blind?" The question really is, Would plaintiff Joe No Name Smith receive equal justice against the State of New York as he or she would receive as against defendant Adam No Name Sue?

When the question is posed, "Is justice blind?" The question really is, would plaintiff Joe No Name Smith received an equal and fair trial against defendant Sally No Name Smith as plaintiff Joe No Name Smith would receive if the defendant was State of New York? Would defendant Sally No Name Smith be afforded the same legal protections as the defendant State of New York?

While most people may already be aware that deep pockets can purchase better legal representation, not enough attention is given to the fact that in many instances, the legal advantages given to governmental entities, such as cities, counties, and states are also wrong. There is usually enough discretion allowed in the law to reach a just decision. In the case at bar, the belief is that the courts are protecting the State and in so doing are seeking to minimize the liability for the financial wrongs committed by a wrongful prosecution. The State of New York is being protected by the New York State Court System from the knowingly wrongful actions taken by State employees in a failed political prosecution. Both the interests of justice and judicial economy require a ruling or decision from the Court of Appeals. Justice delayed is justice denied. Judicial economy would have also required a decision by the Court of Appeals to lessen the number of cases in the court system, not bottleneck the system so that fewer complaints of citizens can be addressed. Time is the court's most valuable resource, and the actions of the court have now decreed that thousands more hours of judicial level time must be expended to determine results in matters in which one of the parties has not objected to the relief requested.

CHAPTER TWELVE

DUTY TO MAKE WHOLE: FACT OR FICTION

After my acquital, the State had a legal duty to make me whole. The idea of making one whole means to restore an individual to the position or lifestyle or a similar situation that the individual enjoyed prior to the commencement of the legal action. In my case, not only did the State refuse to make me whole but instead utilized every and all sorts of vindictive acts against me with the continued direct intent of destroying my business, my practice, and my reputation in the community.

It is clear that the actions were undertaken by government employees under the now revealed corrupt leadership of individuals at the top of the hierarchy, the attorney general of the State and the county executive of the County. Lower-level employees holding position of authority after a failed political prosecution refuse to acknowledge that the actions taken by them were wrong because they were not fired or charged, only their bosses were. The dishonest acts of the lower officials remain in their quest to climb ever higher in the government ladder of power and authority.

The political agenda clearly has not subsided.

After my October 23, 2015, trial jury acquittal, I had been reinstated to receive assignments in the Tioga County assigned counsel program and from a few small towns and villages in upstate New York. The small trickle of cases was abruptly ended by the chief justice of the Appellate Division Third Department, Karen Peters, calling the administrative judge for the Sixth Judicial District and orally ordering that judge to stop all assignment to me in her district.

The depth of the depravity of failed political prosecution is hard to fathom. Justice Peters has taken early retirement from her position, taking full state benefits and retirement before her role in this sordid tale has been able to be brought to the light of day by publication.

From a human perspective, Justice Peters clearly took her actions to finish the criminal prosecution that she had failed in, with enforcement of a civil penalty designed and implemented by her, without the slightest shred of due process of law, fairness, or integrity. Justice Peters wrongfully made a phone call to a Broome County Supreme Court Judge, ordering her, or telling that judge to call Tioga County Family Court to stop assigning any new cases to me. Although it cannot be confirmed, it's my belief that this message was conveyed to all of the courts in the three adjoining counties, Broome County, Tioga County and Delaware County. To have the judge at the top of the organizational hierarchy chart declare someone to be not eligible to receive work is an economic dagger to the heart.

The question that begs to be asked is simply, "Why?"

The answer is three headed.

The first cause is power. As the wisdom of our ancestors states, absolute power corrupts. Judges who have no accountability for their actions do not care whether their actions are legal because they are not accountable for their actions. Power corrupts; absolute power corrupts absolutely.

The second cause is the human frailty of vindictiveness. Judge Peters was about to retire and knew that she would be allowed to fire the final shot with no chance for any response by the victim of her misdeed, your writer.

The third cause is again basic human nature. Judge Peters wanted the last word and knew that she would be able to have it without any consequences to her bank account or reputation.

Justice Peters's acts put the spotlight on her as someone who, instead of aspiring to the lofty goals inscribed on our monuments glorifying justice, just is enamored by the power that she is allowed to wield and whose wielding of that power was done for purposes not in keeping the oath of office that she had sworn to. Judge Peters retired four years prior to the expiration of her duly elected term. Judge Peters played an instrumental role in the failed political prosecution but had escaped the hangman's noose in no small part because the actors in authority above her with whom she collaborated and conceived the prosecution were brought to justice. Despite her political aspirations, Judge Peters wrong thinking and willingness to follow bad decisions made by those higher in authority than her may have contributed to her early retirement.

My race and national origin were doubtless a factor in the original decision to start the prosecution in the first place. The cultural bias of actually giving a black man proper recompense for the wrongs committed against him by the white majority cannot be overstated.

My current lawsuit against the State of New York encompasses slander, libel, and defamation of a business's good name against the State. It is also my belief that the State knows that I am correct but is searching for a way out to be able to save face. It is my belief that saving face has become more important to the State than justice to all. When the goal is to save face and not to have justice, justice cannot be given. When the State takes a knowing position to not seek justice for its citizens, it is the State and every citizen that is wronged.

CHAPTER THIRTEEN

THE COVERUP CONTINUES: COMPLAINTS TO THE STATE COMMISSION ON JUDICIAL CONDUCT

I filed a judicial complaint with the Committee on Judicial Conduct against Hon. Karen Peters and was informed that the commission lacked jurisdiction over Hon. Karen Peters because she had already retired.

Further Background on Post-Trial Retaliation/Reprisal and Abuse of Power by Elected Judges of the New York State Court System

In October 2012, the State of New York wrongfully obtained a warrant and seized 344 of my clients' files from my law office. I was wrongfully accused of overbilling the State of New York and County of Broome for legal work performed for law guardian cases, administered by the Supreme Court Appellate Division Third Department for law guardian cases and the County of Broome for assigned counsel cases for other civil and criminal matters. These wrongful accusations resulted in a one-week trial in Broome County Court from October 19, 2015, to October 23, 2015. I was acquitted of all charges by an all-white Broome County jury. After the verdict, one member of the jury approached and expressed amazement of the actions taken by New York State.

After my acquittal, I wrote to the chief administrative judge of the New York State Office of Court Administration, Hon. Lawrence K. Marks, and the chief administrative judge of the Supreme Court of the State of New York, Third Judicial Department, Michael Coccoma. My letter requested the following:

1. Rescind their prior letter/orders, which had been issued without due process or notice, hence paying me for all legal work performed, unbilled, and unpaid.

2. Reinstatement to the all assigned counsel panels of which I had been a member.

3. The courtesy of a copy of the letter/order showing that the action had been taken.

The judges, to date, have not responded at all to that request.

On December 15, 2015, approximately two months after my acquittal, a copy of the letter was mailed to the chief administrative judge of the New York State Office of Court Administration and the chief administrative judge of the Supreme of the State of New York, Third Judicial Department to the presiding justice of the New York State Supreme Court Appellate Division, Third Department, Hon. Karen K. Peters. About two weeks after my letter to the presiding justice of the New York State Supreme Court Appellate Division, Third Department, I received a letter from the state comptroller making allegations concerning issues that were a part of the criminal trial just concluded. The letter from the state comptroller was dated the very same date of my letter to the chief judge of the New York State Supreme Court Appellate Division, Third Department. This confirmed to me that the State of New York knew of their wrongful conduct and that they were now seeking to partake in further retaliatory actions against me for matters which had been presented to the jury and had been dismissed. Their actions clearly showed that these State employees are of the belief that they are above the law, that the law applies to other people but not to themselves. The actions of the judges show that they are the bad actors that have no respect for the law and/or believe themselves to be above the law.

As of today, The former Chief Judge of the Appellate Division of the Supreme Court of the State of New York, the chief administrative judge of the Appellate Division of the Supreme Court of the State of New York, and the chief administrative judge of the New York State Office of Court Administration have not responded to my written request for the most essential element of justice—fairness and corrective actions for wrongs committed to be taken. The failure of the three judicial officers to take any steps to follow the law confirms the old proverb, "What you do speaks so loud, I cannot hear what you say." Failure to act is the face of knowing wrong is acceptance and confirmation of knowing wrong.

CHAPTER FOURTEEN

LESSONS LEARNED

The biggest and maybe most important lesson learned from my seven years of tribulation is that respect must be earned. The holding of an office does not bestow upon an individual morality. Respect the office, but please require the individual to earn your respect. Respect is meaningful only when it is earned.

One of my old army buddies said to me, "The reason they did that to you is because they do not know who you are." My friendship with that enlisted man hailed back thirty years. The implication here, as I listened to my friend, is that those folks who conspired against me from their high-paying fancy-titled offices were just average people who had never spent a lifetime in service to others. They were simply people who got their paycheck and forgot about the world when their office door closed behind them on Friday night at 4:30 PM. Their belief is that everyone must be average just like them. To that, I say, "I do not care if they know who I am . After all they most likely are not worth it."

I can recall during one of my visits to my native island of Grenada, the island nation that President Ronald Reagan invaded in 1983, a very close family member said to me, "John, you are an unusually strange and different individual." I quickly inquired of her why she made that assessment of me. She replied, "You do not pay much attention to people and what they say or think. That translates to mean it is very difficult for anyone to keep you down or hold you back. This could also be a bad thing or trait, because you would not be aware of when individuals are plotting against you." This, according to her, is my strength in this world but is also my weakness. No one would be able to dissuade or discourage you, but also you would not be aware when people are plotting against you.

Hindsight is always twenty-twenty. My first lawyer in my case told me that "everyone in Broome County knew that they were planning and plotting against you. How did you not know it?" The answer to that question is very simple. When someone has nothing to hide, there is no reason to be looking over one's shoulders. I knew that I was right, innocent, and had nothing to hide, so why worry?

As I conclude this, my seventh book, my first to be published, my hope is that it was objective to the reader. My advice to you is to never cower down to corrupt individuals in so-called high places. Just remember what is said in the Bible, "Lies can be a throne, truth on scaffold, truth will always be victorious over lies." Please always remember that biblical statement as you journey through life. Please do not bow down to people in high government offices. Those who have achieved so-called greatness through wicked and dishonest means never keep it. The sacrifice of integrity is never worth it. It is also my sincere hope that nothing in this book conveys to the reader that I am an angry individual. I was once very angry over this entire affair and chain of events, but I have gotten over it. Today I am at peace, and it is my desire that such peace is displayed in all my writing and forthcoming but yet-to-be-released books.

www.ingramcontent.com/pod-product-compliance
Lightning Source LLC
LaVergne TN
LVHW081546060526
838200LV00048B/2229